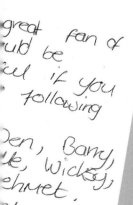

5/6/88

Dear Eastenders

    I am a great fan of your programme. I love it so much that I want to ask you a favor. Please may I have all your autographes and a picture. Thank-you very much I hope you will do my favour.

Lots
of
Love
Samantha
White
(age 10)

great fan of
uld be
ful if you
following

en, Barry,
e, Wickey,
ehmet,
ely

£3.75
1989 edition

EastEnders is a trademark of
The British Broadcasting Corporation.

© The British Broadcasting Corporation 1988.
By arrangement with BBC Publications, a division of BBC Enterprises Ltd.

Photographs from series ©1988 The British Broadcasting Corporation.

Edited by *John Barraclough* and *Morag Bain*. Editorial Assistant: *Jayne M. Lanigan*.
Layout and design: *Nigel I. Money*. Written by *Tony Lynch* and *Morag Bain*. Photographs used in
feature, *Julia Smith's Scrapbook*, supplied by Julia Smith from her own private collection.

Published by
GRANDREAMS LIMITED,
Jadwin House, 205/211 Kentish Town Road,
London NW5 2JU.

Printed in Spain

ISBN 0 86227 626 8

Contents

Judith Jacob & Aisha.

EastEnders Star Portrait - *Dr. Legg & Dr. David.*

EastEnders Star Portrait - *Cindy.*

The Problems of Costumes & Continuity.

EastEnders Star Portrait - *Matthew.*

EastEnders Star Portrait - *Mehmet & Guizin.*

Julia Smith's Scrapbook.

EastEnders Star Portrait - *Sue & Ali Osman.*

EastEnders Star Portrait - *Junior.*

June Brown alias *Dot Cotton.*

EastEnders Star Portrait - *Roly & Willy.*

EastEnders Star Portrait - *Sharon & Michelle.*

Secrets of the Make-Up Department.

EastEnders What You Ask!

EastEnders Star Portrait - *Ian*

'Acting, Rod and Me,' by *Christopher McHallem.*

A Butcher's At Cockney Rabbit & Pork.

EastEnders Star Portrait - *Shireen & Sohail.*

Nick Berry.

Judith Jacob & Aisha

They are probably the most famous mother and daughter acting team on television at the moment. Judith plays Carmel the health visitor and Aisha plays her niece, funnily enough also called Aisha.

Judith is an old hand at the acting game, she started to be interested when she was about thirteen. She had a friend who went to the Anna Scher children's theatre school in the evenings and Judith decided that she'd like to go there too. When she got there she discovered that you could actually act for a living.

The whole thing snowballed from there and it wasn't long before she had her first part and the essential Equity card. By the time she was seventeen she'd been in a variety of productions including *Jumping Bean Bag* and *The Gentle Touch*.

While she was doing her 'A' levels she was asked to audition for *Angels* the hospital series produced by Julia Smith. She went along to the audition with her tall, beautiful friend who was also auditioning.

The decision was eventually between those two good friends. Judith prepared herself for the fact

that her friend was going to get the job, so it came as something of a shock when she learned that she had got the part. She was thrilled and enjoyed working on it very much.

After *Angels* she joined the Black Theatre Co-op doing a play called *Trojans*. This was a new and exciting experience for Judith. From there the company went on to produce more plays and play readings. Judith became more and more involved with the company and now is their Literary Manager as well as being on the board of directors. This means a lot of extra work for Judith. On top of her

EastEnders commitments she has to read all the plays submitted to the theatre, comment on them and, if they're good enough, suggest to the company that they put them on. However despite her busy schedule Judith enjoys her involvement with the company.

Aisha was born on May 30th, 1985. Judith had six months off after she was born and then went back to work on a play. It was during this that Julia Smith approached her agent and asked if Judith would be interested in appearing in *EastEnders*.

Aisha visited the Elstree studios with her mum one day. Julia, who had known Judith for years, was delighted to meet Aisha and during her conversation with her asked if she'd like to be in *EastEnders* with her mum.

Now anyone who knows Julia realises that when she says something like that there is a reason

behind it. Judith knew that something was being plotted by Julia. That evening she and Dennis, her husband, talked about what it would mean for Aisha to be in the programme. Judith decided that it was probably best for Aisha if she didn't do it. However, Dennis pointed out that if she was going to have to act with a two year-old it would be better if it was someone who knew her. So the decision was made — if Julia asked then they would say "yes".

They waited and waited. Judith thought that perhaps the idea had been abandoned, then one day Julia asked her if Aisha would play Darren's daughter. So a star was born!

Aisha loves her "acting", in fact it has helped Judith to get her to eat her breakfast. On days when she's due to go into the studios she's told that if she doesn't eat up she can't go. Her plate is soon cleared!

She adores Aaron Carrington who plays her brother, Junior and in fact calls him her brother and friend in real life.

Judith has no ambitions for Aisha to become an actress when she grows up, she'd rather she became a writer or director. There are too many young girls wanting to become actresses and it's a life full of disappointment, especially when you go for a part and don't get it. However, for Judith and for Aisha there has been little disappointment so far.

What Judith will do next she doesn't know. For the time being she's happy playing Carmel and working when she can with the Black Theatre Co-op.

Whatever her next project is it'll be an exciting challenge. Who knows, one day she may be in a play written or directed by Aisha, keeping up the famous mother and daughter tradition.

Dr. LEGG
and Dr. DAVID
Leonard Fenton and
Christopher Reich

CINDY
Michelle
Collins

EastEnders
STAR PORTRAIT

Dressing-up
for wine-bar
opening —

PHOTOGRAPH.

COSTUME NOTES:

LOT

(30) INT. WINE - BAR 7:30 PM

with Wicksy

LOT

(39) INT - WINE BAR 8:25 PM

↳

CHANGES

LOT

(41) INT. WINE. BAR 8:35 PM

↳

Studio
840 PM

Also

(42) - VIC - BAR

Knees - up

Studio
9:00 PM.

(44) - VIC - BAR

↳

- BLACK J...
Rib...
MAT...
15 Den...
BLACK SUE...
BLACK COL...
- PURPLE -
BLACK S...

NOT AS IN photo (own)

The Costume Department have to keep meticulous records to ensure continuity. Here we see a continuity sheet for Cindy (Michelle Collins). Apart from a description of what she should be wearing, Polaroids are taken for visual reference.

Horizontal

skirt.
Tights
Ts —
loop EARRings -

— HAND BAG straw

The problems of
COSTUMES
& CONTINUITY

Each character in *EastEnders* has an entire wardrobe — consisting of work and leisure outfits, footwear, jewellery and accessories. Co-ordinating and controlling the usage and upkeep of all these items is the Costume Department, currently headed by Costume Designer Yves Barre.

"Many of the clothes were gathered by June Hudson, the show's original Costume Designer," said Yves. "They were based on detailed character biographies written by *EastEnders* creators Julia Smith and Tony Holland. Since that time a succession of Costume Designers have further developed the collection."

Yves Barre was born in the Macon region of France. He came to Britain in 1971 to study fine arts. This included three years in theatre design and costume design. He later became assistant to the well-known opera and ballet designer Nicolas Georgiadis, a job which lasted for 5½ years.

Yves joined the BBC in 1986 and worked as an assistant on various productions before becoming Costume Designer on EastEnders.

He says that the work of a Costume Designer in television is "almost exactly opposite to that of a fashion designer. In fashion you are always anticipating what the next 'look' is going to be. In costume design, be it in theatre, films or TV, we are always looking back into various historical periods and into the way fabrics were used".

Obviously, different characters have different costume needs. "The clothes of the young women like Michelle and Sharon have almost completely changed since *EastEnders* started. This reflects the lifestyles of most genuine East End girls. On the whole they are very fashion conscious and will often discard something after about three months and it is often never seen again.

"On the other hand the wardrobe of Dot Cotton has barely changed at all. Everything has been there since Day One — again a reflection of real life."

Suitable clothes are either found in the BBC's vast stockpile of garments or else on visits to East End markets and some High Street stores. "The problem with BBC stock is that the clothes there, which have been used in other productions, are often slightly out of date, and we prefer to keep an eye on topicality especially for the younger characters. So really it is better to visit the markets and so on. While for a character like Pauline Fowler, I'll often go to good old Marks & Spencer for the odd top and so on," said Yves.

Wardrobes for new characters often have to be created in a hurry. "There

-т. EP. 360
CHARACTER:— JOANNE   ARTIST:— PAMELA SALEM

COSTUME

SCENE		
(A) INT. WINE BAR — EARLY A.M.		
		(LOT)
(B) INT. WINE BAR — AM		
(C) INT. WINE BAR.		
(D) INT. WINE BAR.		
(E) INT. WINE BAR — LATE MORNING.		

NO CHANGES —

Photo
_____
3 Piece Suit: | Plain ivory skirt
STRIPED TOP.
MULTi. Coloured JACKET
flesh Coloured Tights —
BLACK HIGH Heels SHOES — Open Toe.

FAKE GLASS | *USUAL WATCH —
BRACELET — Right | Engagement Ring —
WRIST — | Wed — Ring —

BLACK & MARQUE
EARRINGS

was Dr. David recently who came into the series quickly. He is a 40 year-old man who would obviously have a well-established wardrobe. In his case we bought in second-hand clothes — suits, leather jackets and so on — so that when they go on his back it looks as if he has always worn them and doesn't give the impression of having just come from a shop.

"Another method of achieving that lived-in look with new garments is to wash them a couple of times to break the material down a little."

Perhaps Yves Barre's greatest challenge during his costume designing stint on *EastEnders* was the creation of a wardrobe for the character Joanne, portrayed by Pamela Salem. "Joanne was cast very late so we had to put her wardrobe together very quickly. She was the first *EastEnders* character to dress really expensively. And because of her biographical background she had to dress in a continental style, which straightaway narrowed our choice. She is a stylish, sophisticated lady — not 'glitzy' in the way that Angie Watts sometimes was. Joanne's jewellery, for instance, was purposely kept to a minimum.

"She has a natural instinct for clothes and knows exactly what looks right and would never go over-the-top. There is no way in which her look can be slightly wrong — unlike dear Pat Wicks who tries very hard but doesn't always succeed."

An added challenge for Yves and his team was the fact that Joanne would never be seen twice in the same outfit. She always changes for the evening session in the wine bar, as opposed to the lunchtime session. "This meant there had to be a great deal of variety in her wardrobe . . . a lot of mixtures of tops, skirts and jumpers. From seven basic outfits we managed as many as 25 different looks!"

MATTHEW
Steven Hartley

MEHMET and GUIZIN
Haluk Bilginer and
Ishia Bennison

CAFE OSMAN

EastEnders
STAR PORTRAIT

Left: Julia Smith. Series Producer and co-deviser of EastEnders. *Below:* Stratford-upon-Avon where Julia worked when she re-joined the Royal Shakespeare Company.

Julia Smith is the Series Producer as well as the co-deviser of EastEnders. This year a great honour was bestowed on her by the British Academy of Film and Television Arts—she was given the Desmond Davies Award for her contribution to television. This is only given to people who have long and distinguished careers in television and, who it is felt, have really made their mark.

So, how did Julia reach those dizzy heights? Where did she start and how did EastEnders come about? A glance through Julia's scrapbook might answer some of these questions...

Julia Smith started where many people who work in television begin — in the theatre. She went to drama school, the Royal Academy of Dramatic Art, from there she went into stage management working in various repertory companies touring the country.

It's hard work being on the stage management team. There are so many different responsibilities, from making the tea to finding all the props and even prompting the actors when they forget their lines!

The team is always first up in the morning and last to bed at night — all in all a demanding job, but one the young Julia Smith enjoyed and did well.

It wasn't long before her hard work and dedication

JULIA SMITH'S SCRAPBOOK

Below: Julia directing an episode of the popular tv series, *Dr. Finlay's Casebook. Below bottom:* The Director's credit which appears at the end of a tv programme. It is one which has been repeated many times in Julia's illustrious career. *Right:* Julia directing a tv programme from the gallery.

Directed by JULIA SMITH

BBC *COLOUR*

© BBC 1972

paid off, she landed a very good job with the famous Royal Shakespeare Company, working with well-known actors.

It was while working with Laurence Olivier that Julia got her first job in television. She had been asked to go to Paris to stage manage a play which the BBC were to televise. It was there she met a man from the BBC who was in charge of the television production. He was so impressed by her that she was asked to stage manage the play for television, and was immediately flown back to London to set it up.

That was a lucky break for Julia and a very exciting start to a long and interesting career in television, though at the

time she had no idea what lay ahead. Like everyone in the theatre business she never knew where or when her next job would be.

Julia worked as an assistant floor manager on a variety of productions and it wasn't long before she wanted to make the next step in her career and become a production manager, but in those days it was very difficult for a woman in television — only men became production managers.

So, Julia decided to leave the BBC and go back to working in the theatre. She joined the Royal Shakespeare Company again and went to work in Stratford-upon-Avon. It was while working there that the BBC contacted her and

asked her to go back to work for them as a production manager (during her time away from the BBC the first female production manager had been appointed). So Julia went back to work on classic serials like Pride and Prejudice.

The next step in her career was to do the BBC director's training course and then to become a director. It wasn't long before she was directing the very popular series Dr. Finlay's Casebook, a job she thoroughly enjoyed. While she was directing this she first worked with Patrick Troughton, who was later to play Dr. Who.

One day she was filming with Patrick playing the local schoolmaster

when a funny thing happened. Julia was driving back from the film location when she was stopped by the local policeman. She was a bit puzzled because he looked very serious and she couldn't think what she had done wrong.

He asked her if she was Julia Smith, to which she replied "yes". He then said he was pleased to see what she looked like as his little girl, who was very pretty, had come home from school and said she'd been chosen to be in Dr. Finlay's Casebook by Julia Smith who had said "She'll do, she's nice and ordinary". Fortunately the policeman thought it was quite funny and he let Julia go!

Her first taste of soap opera came next for Julia, she directed episodes of two different programmes, Compact, about a magazine, and The Newcomers which was a bit like EastEnders in that it was about a community and the people living in it.

It wasn't long before Julia was working on the very popular series Dr. Who and in fact she directed the first ever change of Doctors. The first Doctor was played by an actor called William Hartnell, a lovely old man adored by everyone. Following him into the shoes of 'The Doctor' was Patrick Troughton.

One of the stories was set in Cornwall and was all about smugglers and pirates, all very exciting stuff. Some funny sights were to be seen by the local people as the BBC cast and crew went about the filming. The normally quiet village was transformed by the design team into an old fishing village where it wasn't uncommon to see a pirate walking down the main street listening to the cricket on his transistor radio and protecting his wig from the wind and rain with a plastic rainhood. If the villagers looked out to sea they could watch the pirate ship in full sail with a large number of its pirate crew hanging over the side being seasick!

After Dr. Who Julia directed many different programmes, Z Cars, a police series on which she first worked with Tony Holland, Spytrap, and a programme about Alexander Graham Bell, the man who invented the telephone.

Then she made The Railway Children, this was one of her favourites, working with children and wonderful steam engines. Jenny Agutter was in the serial and later went on to make the still-popular film.

After The Railway Children came Angels, the hospital series. Julia first worked on it as a director then later became its producer. This was when her long and successful partnership with Tony Holland really took off.

There are many funny stories from Angels days. One in particular involves the character Rose Butchins played by Kathryn Apanowicz. Rose had just spilt up with her boyfriend. A kind patient had given her a box of chocolates which she stored in her locker. The final scene was of Rose coming off duty, going to her locker, taking out the box of chocolates and

Top left: A scene from the tv series, *Alexander Graham Bell*.
Above top: Julia discusses a point with two members of the cast
of *The Railway Children* and *above:* a scene from the series.

starting to cry.

The assistant floor manager had ordered two boxes of chocolates just in case anything happened to the one on the set.

During rehearsals the scene went well. The director prepared to record the scene. Julia, as producer, had a brilliant idea. She went into the studio gallery and whispered into the director's ear. He in turn passed it on to Kathryn. But no one told the assistant floor manager! The scene was recorded and at the very end Kathryn threw the chocolates into the air, every single one flew all over the studio floor. There was a pause. The

This page: Both these pictures are from the BBC TV series, *Angels*. Can you recognise the young Judith Jacob who went on to play Carmel in *EastEnders*? *Right:* Nerys Hughes in the title role in the tv series, *District Nurse*, which was devised by Julia with Tony Holland.

assistant floor manager gave a gasp. Then the production manager announced that there had been a technical problem and they would have to do the scene again.

The assistant floor manager rushed in with a dustpan and brush and took the chocolates away to dust them down in case they had to do the scene a third time! Fortunately the next time they got it. Everyone thought it was very funny, except the assistant floor manager!

District Nurse was Julia's next project and was the first series devised by her and Tony. Nerys Hughes played Megan, a district Nurse practising in Wales in the 1930's. It was very popular with both adults and children who enjoyed Nerys' performance. They also enjoyed the performance of the programme's other star, 'Scratch' the dog. He was cast when he was just a puppy and quickly became a seasoned performer. He was a bit of a mischief-maker and it wasn't difficult to spot where he had been, as he chewed everything in sight!

Then came EastEnders, Julia and Tony wrote the idea down very quickly one evening in a wine bar in Shepherds Bush. But the format didn't just come to them, they had talked about it many times before. After it was accepted there were many years of hard work

and preparation before episode one finally hit the screens.

Those were exciting and happy days for Julia — watching Albert Square take shape, planning the studio sets down to the smallest detail, creating the characters, contracting the writers and actors, and finally recording the episodes.

Many funny things happened during those years. A sound man once criticized the designer for building Albert Square round a railway bridge. He didn't realize the bridge had actually been built by the design team.

The press have often raised a smile in the EastEnders camp. They'll resort to anything to get a story. One woman

journalist even pretended to be having a baby so that she could get into the hospital where they were filming Michelle having her baby.

Roly has supplied a few laughs too. He once was supposed to chase a cat, but just didn't seem interested. Now, whenever he goes past Dr. Legg's surgery he always looks for the cat. The stories are endless, Julia remembers them all.

These have been happy years for Julia, doing what she loves best — making television programmes. It is only right that she should have received her award. However this isn't the end…she's still full of ideas and it won't be long before the next successful programme is in the planning stages. We can only wait and see.

EastEnders STAR PORTRAIT

SUE and ALI OSMAN

Sandy Ratcliff and Nejdet Salih

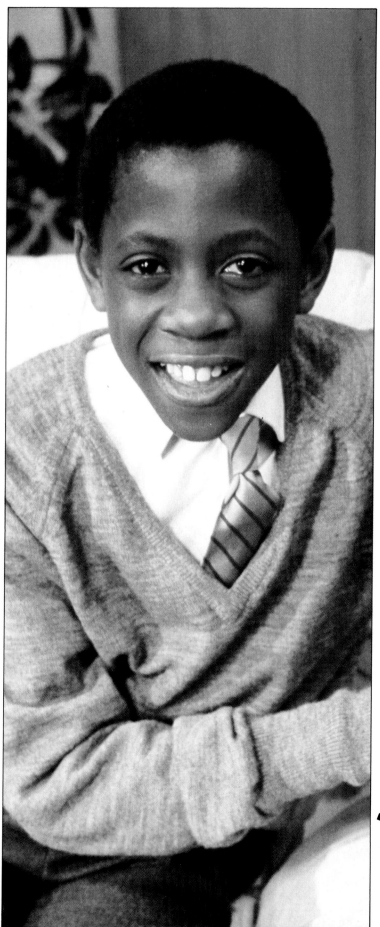

JUNIOR
Aaron Carrington

EastEnders
STAR PORTRAIT

"My favourite Dot Cotton line of all was 'I hope you're satisfied. My Nick's gorn and I've come out in a rash'. I like things like that. I wouldn't mind having just one line per episode if they were all as good as that one," joked June Brown.

June is a lady with a great sense of humour, but admits that she hasn't always been keen to show that side of her nature. "When I first started out in the theatre, I was a very serious young woman, very dramatic. And I used to play those sorts of parts, full of emotion and love. The only time I giggled was when I was nervous or unhappy. But as time goes by you begin to see the funny side of life, and you think 'If only I hadn't taken things so seriously, if only I could have laughed more often.'

"Now of course, thanks to Dot and her constantly miserable, worried expression, people are astonished to see *me* laughing so often!"

June — whose marvellous portrayal of Dot Cotton has won her millions of fans everywhere — first joined the cast of *EastEnders*, episode 40, transmitted in July 1984. "I stood alongside Ethel outside the Queen Vic during the funeral of baby Hassan. I don't think anyone noticed me," she said. "It was a very windy day and my lovely Dot-hairdo got blown about all over the place."

Dot may have gone unnoticed on her Albert Square debut, but that was a situation that would change in future episodes. "Nick Cotton's mother had always

been talked about — right from the start. She lived in the same block of flats as Pete and Kathy Beale and was always doing the *other* shift in the launderette. Originally I had a contract for three months with an option for a further three. Before the first period was up Julia asked me if I would like to become a permanent character.

· "Dot had caught on quickly. I think it happened because she's funny, she amuses people. She is very useful too. In a way she's a peripheral character — she has her own story, but can also be involved in other storylines. Like a carrier-pigeon she can flit from one place to another with her

Left: June Brown as Dot Cotton and right: her screen husband, Charlie, played by Christopher Hancock.

little snippets. I love playing her, but I do have to be careful not to enjoy her too much. If that happened then she might not appear funny to other people."

Unlike poor Dot with her fraught relationships with errant son Nick and often absent husband Charlie, June gets along very well with the two actors who portray the men in Mrs Cotton's life.

"John Altman was in *EastEnders* from the beginning — young Nick was always suspected of murdering Reg Cox. He's a lovely boy and we've always had a laugh and a joke on set together.

"As for Chris Hancock who portrays Charlie — well, I knew him when we were both very young. He went to the same drama school as me — the Old Vic Theatre School. I was actually there before him, but his girlfriend at the time was a friend of a friend of mine and we girls all lived in a flat in Bond Street — so I saw him quite often. He was a very good-looking, rather sensitive young man in those days."

June's real life husband is actor Robert Arnold who was once very familiar to TV viewers as PC Swain in the long-running police series *Dixon of Dock Green*. The rest of her family consists of four daughters; Louise, Sophie, Chloe and Naomi and a son, William, all of them in their twenties. "It's lovely having grown-up

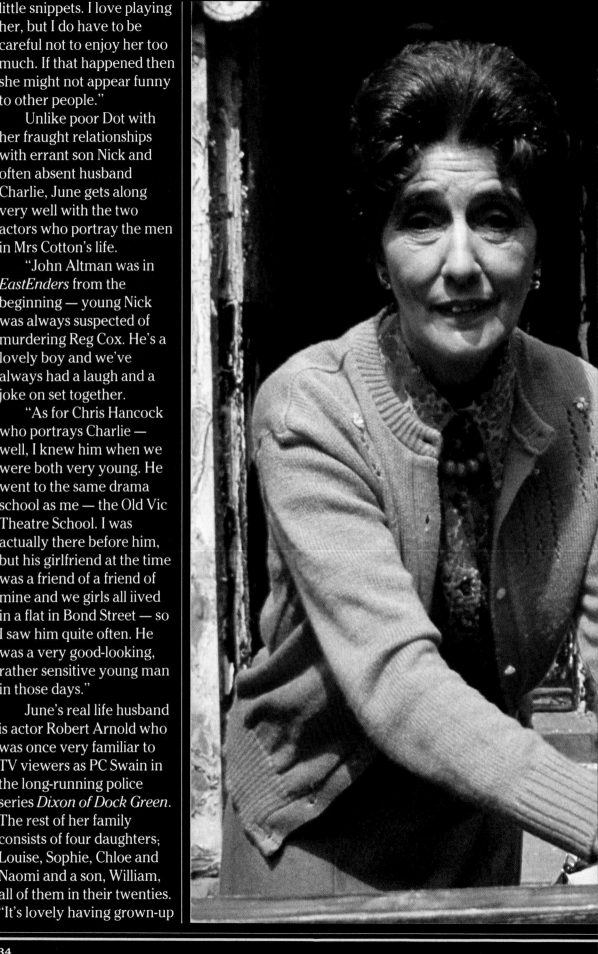

children around," said June.

"Ages ago one of them asked me if I'd like to appear in a soap opera. I wouldn't have been so keen when I was younger. Partly because it was different then — if you did get known as a particular character then it was very difficult to do anything else. It's different now of course. Anyway I watched the soaps because the children did, and of course I got hooked on *Dallas, Dynasty, Crossroads* and *Brookside.* When *EastEnders* first came along I refused to watch it. I thought I simply cannot get hooked on another one! And I didn't actually start to watch it until I knew I was going to be in it. Now I watch it whether I'm in it or not, to see how things are developing. I enjoy it too."

Before *EastEnders* June Brown's face was well-known among that gallant band of brilliant British character artistes who were always popping up on the screen. "I worked in lots of things, for something like 36 years, prior to *EastEnders.* For years I played a lot of sick women — probably because I'm so thin. I was often the 'friend' or the working-class lady in the odd 'cardie'. I was a woman having a nervous breakdown in John Schlesinger's film *Sunday, Bloody Sunday,* I cried all the time in that."

June's favourite role on the stage was as Aurielia Plath, mother of the poet Sylvia Plath in *Letters Home.* "I really loved doing that — it was written as an apologia for Aurielia of whom people had said 'No wonder Sylvia committed suicide with a mother like that'. The play redressed the balance. It was later done as a radio play and a film."

On TV she has been seen in such productions as *The Sweeney, Home and Away, South Riding, Angels, The Duchess of Duke Street, A Christmas Carol, Minder, The Bill,* and *Lace*.

But it is as Dot Cotton that TV fans adore June Brown. For she has managed with consummate professionalism to bring sympathy and humour and a genuine reality to a character who, on the surface, is little more than an interfering busybody. "Dot is far more complex than she appears. She seems inconsequential, but she isn't. She has this constant thread running through her all the time. There is always a reason for what she says — even if it sometimes seems to come out of the blue.

"Basically her intentions are good. She has her own strange brand of Christianity, but she is a true believer which is why we've made sure that people take her faith seriously. I myself don't like to see religion sent up or ridiculed. I'm in sympathy with Dot and I just love playing her as truthfully as I'm able."

ROLY and WILLY

SHARON and MICHELLE

Letitia Dean and Susan Tully

EastEnders STAR PORTRAIT

Secrets of the
MAKE~UP DEPARTMENT

Janet Phillips is a young lady who obviously enjoys her work — in the make-up department of EastEnders. "It was something I always wanted to do, right from my schooldays," she said.

Janet passed A-Level examinations in English, history and art, all essential

"Eventually I wrote to the BBC, asking for information about careers in make-up. They replied by sending me an application form for what is known as the

subjects for the budding make-up artist.

On leaving school she became a beautician working in a salon. But always at the back of her mind was the thought that she would one day like to work in television.

BBC Make-Up School. I applied along with hundreds of others. Then I was invited to take a make-up test and eventually won one of the few places on the two year course."

What followed was three months of intensive training in the art and craft of television make-up techniques at the Make-Up School. And there was a stiff test at the

Janet Phillips, one of two make-up supervising assistants on *EastEnders*, putting the finishing touches to Dot Cotton (June Brown). *Bottom:* Because he is so fair, actor William Boyde, who plays James Willmott-Brown, has to have his eyebrows darkened.

end to judge the students' progress. Janet passed and then took the next step in her career.

"This meant working alongside experienced make-up artists. Just watching them to start with and then gradually becoming more and more involved with the work," said Janet.

Eventually she was promoted to make-up assistant and worked on several historical dramas and a number of situation comedies.

Nowadays she is one of the two

Left: Janet with Dot Cotton (June Brown) and *below:* Carmel (Judith Jacob), seen here with her screen boyfriend Matthew (Steven Hartley), is one of Janet's responsibilities.

Supervising Assistants on the EastEnders *make-up team, based at the show's Elstree headquarters. Other department members are two Make-up Designers and four assistants.*

"I'm now responsible for the hair and make-up needs of my own group of artistes," said Janet. "Among others this includes June Brown, Wendy Richard, Matilda Zeigler, Judith Jacob and William Boyde."

With long established characters such as Dot Cotton and Pauline Fowler, the make-up and hair follows a set pattern. "Although the make-up of any character can alter within the storyline — they may go out somewhere special or may go off for a job interview, or to see the bank manager. In such cases they would naturally spruce themselves up a bit."

New characters are more of a challenge to Janet and her colleagues who, after discussion with the make-up designers, must set to work on the 'look' of the newcomer.

Make-up materials used in EastEnders *are precisely the same as those bought over the counter in any High Street store. "It's rare these days for theatrical make-up to be used in television. With today's cameras being so sophisticated and sensitive, a natural look is imperative. Anything that looks at all theatrical appears way 'over-the-top' on screen. We do, however, apply the base material with sponges and brushes, whereas most girls usually apply their make-up with their fingers."*

Male characters are generally not made-up, or at least will use the minimum of attention. "There are exceptions — William Boyde, for instance, who plays James Willmott-Brown, is so fair that his eyelashes and eyebrows have to be darkened down, otherwise they would practically disappear on screen."

The hairstyle for each character is also the responsibility of the make-up department. "We do cut the hair of certain artistes, while others prefer to go to their own hairdresser, under supervision, of course! However, on a recording day we are responsible for the 'look' of the hair. Sometimes, this means the creation of a wig, although not very often."

Special make-up effects are sometimes called for by the storyline. A black eye, for instance, or perhaps some other wound. "When this happens we not only have to produce the desired affect, we also have to take into account just how long *the effect will last. A black eye will heal gradually over the course of a few episodes, while a more serious wound might take a lot longer to heal. Whatever the situation these wounds must appear to repair themselves naturally."*

Even the non-human members of the EastEnders *cast cannot escape the attentions of the make-up department. "If Roly, the dog, goes astray, then we have to dirty him down like any dog who has wandered the streets for any length of time!"*

Of course, the major problem for make-up — as with most other departments on EastEnders, *is that of continuity. "Because scenes are shot out of order we have to keep a file of careful notes on each character. We also take a lot of Polaroid photographs to use as reference material. One day it will be fun to look back and see just how the 'look' of the* EastEnders *changed and evolved."*

THE MAKE~UP GALLERY

With scenes quite often "shot" out of sequence, it is vital that a record is kept of each character's make-up. To assist her, Janet Phillips uses Polaroid pictures. Here we see some of those pictures taken of the artistes Janet is responsible for.

PAULINE FOWLER
(Wendy Richard)

DOT COTTON (June Brown)

Left to right: DUNCAN (David Gillespie), **MATTHEW** (Steven Hartley), **CARMEL** (Judith Jacob)

DONNA (Matilda Ziegler)

JAMES WILLMOTT-BROWN (William Boyde)

"What is your starsign?"

"What was your favourite book at school?"

"Do you wear your own clothes or are they specially bought for the programme?"

"Please, please, please can I be in EastEnders?"

"We are having a charity auction, do you have anything you could donate for it?"

"What's your favourite t.v. programme?"

"Can I please have your autograph?"

"Where can I buy the clothes you wear?"

"Are you from a big family? Do you have any brothers or sisters?"

"Would you like to come to my house for tea?"

"Have you any pets?"

EastEnders
WHAT YOU ASK!

EastEnders, being the number one television programme, receives sackloads of mail each week. They are mainly letters from fans writing to their favourite stars; ranging from cards and letters to drawings and gifts, all requiring a reply. A team of secretaries sorts through the mail daily, dealing with simple requests for photographs and autographs and then making up bundles of letters for the personal attention of each star. Fans eager for information usually ask the same questions, and here you can see a selection of the most popular requests.

"Do you get on with the other members of the cast?"

"Please can you sign the enclosed birthday card for my sister?"

"Do you have a fan club?"

"Do you have a favourite recipe?"

"PLEASE can I visit Albert Square?"

"What is your date of birth?"

"Have you always wanted to be an actor/actress?"

"What's your favourite colour?"

"Who is your favourite actor/actress?"

"Do you have any hobbies?"

"What did you do before EastEnders?"

"Can I please have some signed beermats from the Queen Vic?"

IAN~Adam Woodyatt

EastEnders
STAR PORTRAIT

'Acting, Rod and me,' by CHRISTOPHER McHALLEM

Christopher McHallem who portrays Rod Norman the ex-roadie in **EastEnders**, was born 28 years ago and was brought up in west London . . .

HOW DID YOU GET THE PART OF ROD?

I was originally supposed to play the part of a drugs dealer in just one episode. It was the time when the Queen Vic was going downhill, when the place was full of young tearaways. I met Mike Gibbon who was then a director. He sent me to see Julia Smith and Tony Holland who told me they'd created a new character and asked if I would like to play him. Rod had apparently been 'hanging around' Albert Square for sometime and had been noticed by Mary.

DID YOU HAVE TO AUDITION?

Not in the true sense of the word. I just sat there while they talked to me about the character. I suppose they were looking for someone close to their idea of Rod and I assume they saw certain of his qualities in me. They have to work like that because of the pace of the show. If an actor had to spend too much time looking for his 'motivation' and feeling his way into the role, then he'd soon find his P45 in his pay packet.

DO YOU REMEMBER YOUR FIRST LINES AS ROD?

He was sitting in the square with some others, a policeman approached to move them on and Rod responded by saying: "Hang about. It's a free country anyway."

YOU WERE RATHER THROWN IN AT THE DEEP END . . .

True. Although the work didn't really come as a shock as I've seen happen with some other people. I came in all innocence and imagined that all television programmes were produced at such a hectic pace. I didn't stop to worry about it.

Of course, it's impossible for me to compare yet, but I imagine if you're working in a TV play then you work hard for two or three weeks, and then it's all over. But because of the nature of EastEnders *the pressure is seemingly endless. I'm used to it now that I've found my feet. I like the fact that the 'end' isn't written.*

IS IT DIFFICULT TO SHOOT SCENES OUT-OF-SEQUENCE?

It can be. But really it's a matter of going back to the script and making notes whenever necessary. Often we do 'double-banking' which means you're working on several different episodes at a time. Leslie Grantham was once working on bits of fourteen *at the same time. I think I'd find that a bit daunting. Luckily my part has been fairly straightforward so far.*

DO YOU LIKE ROD AS A PERSON?

There are obviously enormous differences between our reactions to certain things. But, yes, I like him. I think I like him more than he'd like me. I wonder if he'd watch EastEnders — I doubt it somehow, he'd probably watch Brookside!

He's a mass of contradictions. People often ask 'How come he did that?' or 'Why did he do that?' But that's real. People aren't simply good or bad.

Someone described him to me as a pragmatist. I nodded knowingly then asked Leonard Fenton what it meant. Leonard said it was someone who lives for the moment and takes the chance. Which is absolutely right for Rod. He has a fairly fluid morality. He'll get by.

WHAT ARE YOUR FEELINGS ABOUT HIS RELATIONSHIP WITH MARY?

It was a shame that it didn't work out for him. It was a good storyline — one which went full circle. On their last episode together they seemed to be talking in a way they never had before — very openly, about themselves and the fact that it just wasn't going to work out.

I remember when we did the big bust-up scene. I came home and watched something on video tape. At the end of it was the first episode in which Mary and Rod were together. It was quite sad, seeing it again.

HOW DID YOU BECOME AN ACTOR?

I'd had hundreds of jobs. I'd tried all the things I thought I wanted to do and then realised I didn't want to do them after all. One of the people who lives near me was at the Central Drama School and they suggested that I audition for a place.

I'd done Shakespeare and other plays at school, but had never really considered acting as a career. I didn't know where actors came from — I certainly didn't think they were people like me.

Anyway, I prepared my audition pieces and went along expecting to see these terrible ogres calling petrified people onto the stage. But it wasn't as frightening as I'd imagined. It was really quite informal and enjoyable.

Eventually I heard that I'd been accepted and was given a grant to go there.

HOW LONG WAS THE COURSE AND WHAT DID IT ENTAIL?

Three years, six days a week. You have classes in all sorts of relevant subjects: voice, dance, tap, jazz, fencing, stage fighting and make-up (at which I was particularly awful!).

Each term you are working on a different play. These include a Chekhov, a Shakespeare, a restoration piece, a modern American play, a Shaw or a Coward, an Ibsen and then another Shakespeare. In this way you get to delve into everything from comedy to tragedy. And you get to discover your own strengths and weaknesses. It also gives you a knowledge of the incredible scope of theatre.

During the first two years you are involved in one-off productions which are seen by the other students. Then at the end of the third year comes a five nights production at Central's Embassy Theatre. This is when the agents and casting people and the mums and dads come to see you.

WHEN DID YOU LEAVE CENTRAL — AND WHAT HAPPENED NEXT?

I left in 1986. Then I was asked by Lawrence Boswell if I'd like to join his company — The Pocket Theatre Co — who were producing Can't Pay, Won't Pay *in Cumbria. Lawrence had worked on*

Ibsen's A Doll's House *during my second year at Central.*

I was very lucky to find work straight away. Some of my old classmates are beginning to get established now, but one or two have given up trying.

I later went back to Cumbria to play Claudio, Elbow and Fr. Peter in Measure for Measure. *I also did a couple of things in films. But between leaving drama school and joining* EastEnders *I also spent several months on the dole. It really can be a tough and frustrating life.*

WHAT ABOUT YOUR

FAMILY — WERE THEY SURPRISED WHEN YOU BECAME AN ACTOR?

Not really. My mum had never said 'Don't be daft, you'll never be an actor'. Whenever I said I'd be late home from school because I was rehearsing the school play, she didn't try to discourage me. On the other hand when I told her I wanted to be a footballer she said 'Don't be so stupid'. She knew I didn't have the makings of a professional soccer player. I still think I should have been a footballer — Chelsea need me now.

YOU STILL PLAY

THOUGH, FOR THE WALFORD BOYS' CLUB . . .

Yes — it's our charity team. We've played at some really big grounds Villa Park, Preston North End and so on. That's like a dream come true.

WHAT DOES THE FUTURE HOLD FOR ROD?

He's got plans. Whether they work out or not, we'll just have to wait and see. But whatever happens I'm sure he'll survive.

. . . AND FOR YOU?

I'm a bit pragmatic, like Rod. So I'll get by too.

A BUTCHER'S AT COCKNEY RABBIT & PORK

Cockney Rhyming Slang is as old as London herself. It has evolved over the centuries as different cultures have influenced the language of the greatest capital city of them all.

Here is an imaginary — and far-fetched — passage that might be spouted by my old mate, Pete Beale.

And for those readers who live North of Watford, East of Essex, West of Windsor or South of Surrey — don't worry, there's a translation to follow.

66 'ere, Arthur. I was right peeved this morning. I took a cup of ROSY up the APPLES to give to mum, cause she was feeling a bit TOM. I puts the cup on the CAIN all quiet and gentle like, when mum suddenly sits up in bed and gives me a right old BUTCHER'S. She fixed me with her MINCES and then opened her NORTH AN' SOUTH.

"'ere," she says. "'ave you been down the RUB-A-DUB for a pint of PIG'S?"

"No," I says, all honest and truthful like. Well she didn't believe me, did she. She just went on and on about it. Cor blimey, she can't half RABBIT. I'd soon had enough, I can tell you.

So, I went home, changed me DICKY, put on me WHISTLE, combed me BARNET, put on me TITFER, shoved a handful of BEES in me SKY and then I *did* go down the RUB-A-DUB! 99

Translation:
ROSY = ROSY LEA = TEA
APPLES = APPLES & PEARS = STAIRS
TOM = TOM & DICK = SICK
CAIN = CAIN & ABEL = TABLE
BUTCHER'S = BUTCHER'S HOOK = LOOK
MINCES = MINCE PIES = EYES
NORTH AN' SOUTH = MOUTH
RUB-A-DUB = RUB-A-DUB-DUB = PUB
PIG'S = PIG'S EAR = BEER
RABBIT = RABBIT & PORK = TALK
DICKY = DICKY DIRT = SHIRT
WHISTLE = WHISTLE & FLUTE = SUIT
BARNET = BARNET FAIR = HAIR
TITFER = TIT-FOR-TAT = HAT
BEES = BEES & HONEY = MONEY
SKY = SKY ROCKET = POCKET

SHIREEN & SOHAIL
Nisha Kapur & Ronny Jhutti

NICK BERRY

Nick Berry is undoubtedly one of the most popular young actors on television today, thanks to his marvellous portrayal of Simon Wicks in EastEnders — a character who has grown and developed with the series.

Although his name had been put forward during the planning stages of the programme by his agent, Sylvia Young, Nick actually joined the cast some three months after EastEnders had begun broadcasting. For a while he had believed he might never become an Albert Square regular!

Luckily for Nick — and for fans of EastEnders — the part of 'Wicksy' was created and the role just had to be filled. Nick Berry fitted the bill perfectly.

N ick Berry was born in Woodford Green, Essex, the son of a sales representative and the second in a family of four children.

He first attended Woodford Green Primary school and was educated there until the family moved home to Manor Park in East London.

His next school was Aldersbrook where he stayed until moving on to Wanstead Comprehensive.

He has described himself as an 'average' pupil who was mad about sport — especially soccer.

In fact, he was a good enough footballer to represent East London Boys, in the same team as current Wimbledon ace, Terry Gibson. So, Nick might well have followed in the footsteps of many other East End lads with talent in their boots, and become an apprentice with a professional football club.

However, there was another facet to his personality — he was decidedly *stagestruck*. He appeared in school productions and attended the Sylvia Young Theatre School in the evenings and at weekends.

His photogenic good looks won him parts in several TV commercials — for chocolate bars, fruit pastilles and even hamburgers! These were paid jobs and must have made the prospect of a career before the cameras a very attractive one indeed.

At the age of 14, Nick was offered the role of one of Fagin's urchins in a touring production of the famous musical *Oliver!* After consultation with his parents he accepted the job.

This meant leaving school for the duration of the tour — but attending special lessons so that his education would not suffer.

For almost a year, young Nick toured the length and breadth of Britain with the *Oliver!* company. When the run ended he returned home and went back to Wanstead Comprehensive to sit his CSE exams (achieving passes in maths, metalwork, English and, guess what? *Drama*).

By this time he had realised that the world of show-biz might be a decidedly insecure occupation to follow. So, he found himself a job in the world of publishing — as an assistant librarian on a magazine called *Petroleum Economist*.

This lasted for a year and a half — but the entertainment bug had bitten deep and Nick auditioned for a part in a production of the Greek tragedy *Orestes*. He won the role and next day handed in his notice at the magazine office.

Later came small roles on television in such programmes as *Dramarama, The Gentle Touch* and *Cover Her Face.*

Nick made his film debut in *Party Party,* a low-budget production which received good reviews and instilled in him the ambition to make more movies in the future.

Nick was involved in the West End production of a play called *Why Me?* at the Strand Theatre when the offer of the part of 'Wicksy' came along. As we now know, he leapt at the chance, and has never looked back.

Since gaining fame in *EastEnders*, Nick Berry has extended his career into other areas — notably appearing in pantomime and, of course, making the Number One smash hit record, *'Every Loser Wins'*, in 1986.

But it is the portrayal of Simon Wicks in *EastEnders* which holds him now. The development of the character is his job, and one that he will continue to do to perfection.

Dear Julia, I am write to say
if   can have signed photos
of the EastEnders and other Information and your Autographs
I have watched EastEnders
since it started. My favourite
star is Den and Frank. It
is a very enjoyable
programe to watch
and I forward
to the next   I have got

P.T.O.

2

Matthew
Stanford

QUeen   Victora

Dear Sir/Madam
    I am
Eastenders an
extremely g
could send m
autographs.
Ian, kathy, Pe
Colin, Sharon,
Duncan, Ali an
    yours

Ray